PLAYTIME: NOT JUST FOR CHILDREN

PLAYTIME: NOT JUST FOR CHILDREN

A GUIDE TO SEXUAL CONQUESTS FOR WOMEN

Amanda Pasciucco, LMFT, AASECT CST

ISBN-13: 9780692821749
ISBN-10: 0692821740

Thank you to my Savior. Without You, I am nothing.

I dedicate this book to my confidant, Leanne Peterson.
Thank you for your vision!

I dedicate this book to my former professor, Jim Moorhead.
You have illuminated my passion.

To my lover, my parents, my brother, my family, my friends, my coworkers, and my clients; your encouragement has led me to believe I have something worth sharing.

Contents

PREFACE

GET READY TO transform your sex life. It is time to open yourself up to new and better relationships with yourself and others. This book takes you through a series of discussions and exercises designed to take you to a new level. It is largely written for monogamous, heterosexual females, but the lesbian, polyamorous, queer, transgender, BDSM, and swinging communities have used these techniques. As with any advice book, open yourself up to my suggestions, but rely on yourself to know what works for you.

CHAPTER 1

THE AUTHENTIC SELF

WOMEN ARE LOSING at the game of sex. As a twenty-eight-year-old woman who is a licensed marriage and family therapist (LMFT) as well as an American Associate of Sex Educators, Counselors, and Therapists (AASECT) certified sex therapist (CST), I find a large part of my therapeutic sessions are devoted to teaching women about femininity, self-love, and achieving pleasure.

Ironically an abundance of sexually charged "chatter" is everywhere we turn—social media, tabloids, romance novels, and movies. Women are reducing themselves to cookie-cutter sexual clones packaged in five-inch stilettos, hair extensions, fake tans, false lashes, and pounds of makeup. These messages keep women pinned as sexual objects and away from being sexually empowered.

In this book I will help reinforce the importance of developing a deep sense of self-worth, which will give you the confidence needed for a fulfilling intimate life with a partner. This book is a guide for women getting started on their journey of sexuality. I want to make sure *you*, my reader, don't end up in a place where you are not satisfied with your sexual life.

My goal is for you to learn the art of self-love and the rewards of accepting your body at a young age. I will do this by sharing the relevant information in a format that suits your individual needs. This chapter is a primer regarding authenticity, acceptance, and self-love that will provide the foundation for the rest of the book. It is my hope that early on you will start thinking differently about yourself, your body, and your romantic relationships. After the introductory chapter, each chapter provides guidance on specific topics that come up regularly in my counseling sessions.

Once you let go of erroneous thoughts regarding intimacy and sexuality, you can develop mature, realistic perspectives regarding acceptance, self-love, intimacy, and *physical pleasure*. From this place of acceptance, I will discuss and guide you in the importance of positive self-talk, as well as how to have an open, honest dialogue with your partner. Together you can discuss new techniques and methods with openness, which I believe will take you to a new world of pleasure and fulfillment.

LET'S TALK ABOUT SEX

What is great sex, anyway? Given all that I have read and experienced in the realm of sexuality, I have been asked this question time and time again. If it was a one-sentence answer, I probably would have saved a lot of relationships by now. The thing is that with sexuality, many components are factors. What I have learned is that sexuality is the combination of a physical, intellectual, spiritual, and emotional connection with another. What does this mean? I will explain below.

Physical: I believe that the most books I have read about sex are those about how to have a good physical connection. You learn the physical techniques and how to pursue someone you're interested in using your skill. However, being confident in your sexual repertoire is just one component of great sex. In this book we will discuss physical techniques, but please know that different people have different physical preferences. Just remembering some specific physical suggestions can be helpful, but this only makes up a quarter of what I believe is needed in great sex.

Intellectual: You and the person you want to engage in sexual activity with should be able to discuss intentions, thoughts, desires, fears, and concerns that you have with one another. Oh, and by the way, it would be great to do this *before* you get into any sexual act with this person. This may sound crazy to some of you, I know. (I have been told by clients many times throughout my therapy and teaching sessions that *this is not how the world works* or that *nowadays, the random hookup just happens, and there's no prenegotiation or follow-up*.) Sometimes the energy connection is so strong that you don't even need words or intellectual compatibility to achieve high levels of sexual excitement or fulfillment. I believe a slight chance exists you could stumble into good sex this way. But the best choice would be to negotiate boundaries and discuss desires with the person with whom you are going to engage in sex prior to having a sexual experience. This may sound foreign to some of you, but to some people, especially within the BDSM community, this type of prenegotiation is a regular part of the sexual exchange.

Spiritual: For some of you, this might sound scary. What do I mean by spiritual? It's almost like having a runner's high or the rush that you get from the wind blowing in your face while driving on a nice day. This is the realm of deep understanding and connection to something that is greater than the hookup. I believe that spiritual component is the union of the souls within the sexual experience—the *juice* of great sex. This connection and desire to keep exploring the depths of who you are and who you want to be with a partner is somewhat magical. This may sound a little "hippie" to some of you, but when you reach the spiritual connection, you feel the energy travelling through your body.

Emotional: The emotional realm is where you and the person with whom you are connecting have a heart-to-heart bond. This comes in the form of a couple that has been together numerous years, the excitement of new relationship energy, or a deep sexual connection where both of you are open to being vulnerable and sharing your intimate self with the other. The emotional realm is the place where you feel safe with the person you are with. You feel that the other person has your best intentions at heart and vice versa.

BEING IN THE MOMENT

If you are like most people, you may feel anxious or nervous in the dating scene and think negative thoughts about yourself. You may remember all the failed dating attempts you've experienced and the people who have rejected you. When this happens, you must try to come back to the present moment; refocus your attention on centering and grounding yourself. *What does that mean?* It means activating your five senses.

Feel your feet on the ground, notice what you hear, inhale deeply into your stomach, and exhale longer than you inhale. Notice the temperature and scent of the room around you. Once you fully embrace your body, you can look around at your surrounding environment. When you feel that you are mentally in the right place, you will notice that you are filled with more confidence. This ability to be present and in the current moment is an essential part of having amazing sexual experiences.

Remember that going out drinking to meet new people does not work for everyone! If you think, "Something must be wrong with me because I'm not successful in dating," the current dating scene just may not work for you. You may experience anxiety because your way of connecting with others does not fit into the societal norm of meeting at a bar and bringing someone home with you. Feeling as though you must connect and deliver on the first date because that is what you "should" be doing can promote great anxiety. You may feel that something is wrong with you if people don't want to hook up with you after one meeting. Sometimes it may feel as if you should do ritualistic behaviors, such as a random hookup, because that is the common way to connect with others. As hard as it may seem, letting that mind-set go can be freeing. If the dating scene you have been trying hasn't been working for you, you may want to switch it up and attempt something other than meeting a partner in a bar or club.

Remember that if you always do what you have always done, you will always get what you have always gotten. Don't keep approaching a dating situation the same way with the same mind-set and say that dating doesn't work for you. Try new places, develop a new mind-set, and be open to new people. Keep in mind that many millennials are connected to Wi-Fi and phone apps, so maybe it is time to try out online dating! I have seen a ton of success with clients and friends who have met partners online.

Don't Put Pressure on Sex

The most important part of having a great sexual experience is the mentality in which you go into the experience. Anxiety around sex comes from focusing on the outcome of an encounter or a relationship. To relieve this anxiety, you need to focus more on the process of discovering yourself and your partner. The goal is to enjoy the discovery process instead of worrying about the sexual outcome or putting pressure on orgasm. When it comes to encounters and relationships, the most helpful stance to take is one of curiosity. When you are curious, nothing can go wrong since there are no expectations, just discoveries. Everything that happens will provide feedback on what you want moving forward.

When you go into a sexual space feeling confident about your body and open to an emotional connection with your partner, the experience is much more enjoyable. When you are with your partner, it is beneficial to praise and honor the body of the person you are with. Adore the various parts of your partner's body with different sensations and pressures. Let your mind overflow with pleasurable thoughts about being with this person with whom you are sharing a sexual experience. Take time to learn different things that are exciting to the other person and notice the way the person's body responds to your touch. Let your erotic brain fantasize about the person and what he or she may want. When you let your mind do this type of thinking, the body can typically follow. The connection between people in a sexual space can be the most important tool you will need in having awesome sex.

Appreciation and praise are important in your sexual encounters. Appreciating your body is vital. Even if you think your body is not "perfect," keep in mind that it is serving you well. It allows you to hold someone, kiss someone, bring pleasure to someone else, and receive pleasure yourself. It is important to focus on those things and let go of the "I don't look like a model" thoughts. Those types of thoughts will not serve you in this situation, so let go of those old and negative messages. Just as you learn to be kind toward your body, it is important to appreciate your partner's body and let your partner know it. Both women and men can be self-conscious. Knowing that your partner appreciates you and your body helps you be more in the moment, and letting the other person know how much you appreciate him or her allows your partner to be more in the moment with you and enjoy it more.

AUTHENTICITY AND AFFIRMATIONS

Before you move forward with sexual experiences, take an inventory of what you want. As humans we are all influenced by the messages we receive from society. For a long time, the message has been that sex is bad, sex is shameful, sex is not acceptable, and sex is only performed for practical purposes. Secretiveness upholds and fuels the shame that we tend to feel around sex. All these negative feelings about sex are not discussed, processed, or balanced out by positive messages. Sadly, if you feel shame around sex, it can be hard to have honest and frank conversations about it with your partner.

Feeling shame surrounding sex can be normal, but you can change that through open, frank discussion. The first step to releasing these old messages is to arrive at a place where you are willing to let them go. Ask yourself, "Are these messages helping me be a better person or partner? How have these messages gotten in the way in the past? Do I want to believe something different about sex?" Challenge the messages you have that associate shame with sexuality.

Before you can heal from these thoughts, you must move away from the source of what is causing the problems. Assess your mind-set toward your sexuality. Do you have a recording that plays in your head about sexuality without knowing it? Perhaps your recording says something like, "This is wrong. I shouldn't like this. I'm bad for doing this."

We all play recordings with sound bites filled with conflicting information from parents, society, and social circles. The goal is to replace old recordings, which are not enhancing your life, with new ones that serve you better. The first part is recognizing when an old recording is playing; once you recognize it, change your focus to a new one.

A million thoughts enter our minds every day. Do not try to censor and fix every thought that comes into your head. Focus on the thoughts that serve you well and work for you. For example, when the thought, "I am bad for having sex," comes in your head, you are going to switch your focus to a positive affirmation—even if you don't believe it.

Here are some examples of these affirmations:

- I allow myself to experience and enjoy pleasure knowing that I am okay;
- I am a sexual goddess;
- I am worthy of wonderful sexual connection;
- I open my life up to positive sexual experiences;
- I feel confident in my expression of sexuality;
- My sexual power entices others to draw closer to me.

Whatever the old recording is, find a new message that works for you and replay the new one over and over. One day it will be so natural to play the new recording that the old one will no longer repeat.

How to Get on Board with Loving Yourself

You have the potential to be your biggest supporter or your worst critic. The more positive you are about yourself, the more positive your experiences in the world will be. To truly embrace sexuality, we must first truly love ourselves and our bodies. Work on having a positive body image in which you see your body for what it truly is and appreciate its shape. The goal is to feel comfortable when looking at your body—not necessarily loving every single part, but to be accepting of its form. Challenge the negative self-talk associated with your body by utilizing affirmations and positive body statements.

Try This Out

1. *Take some deep breaths; breathe in a positive affirmation, and breathe out a judgment or self-criticism. For example breathe in a thought such as "I am beautiful as I am," and exhale "I hate my thighs."*
2. *Look at yourself when you pass by a mirror and compliment yourself. Imagine talking to yourself as you would talk to a friend.*
3. *Go on walks, call a friend, take a bath, or give yourself some "me time" every day.*

4. *Pick one positive affirmation, and repeat this affirmation to yourself every day for thirty days. An example of this could be "I have a beautiful face."*

5. *Compliment other women on positive characteristics about them that do not have to do with their outward appearance.*

6. *Look at other bodies—not model or porn star bodies, but nude art. Appreciate their natural forms.*

7. *Do not talk negatively about your body, and do not talk about your diet in front of other people.*

8. *See a registered dietician, and go on a meal plan if you feel it is necessary. Learn to eat healthy, and avoid fad diets. Healthy diets lead to healthy bodies.*

9. *Incorporate cardio and yoga (or something you prefer) into your life. Do not overexercise; just get your body moving for about thirty minutes each day.*

10. *Write a top-ten list of what you like about yourself. Read it multiple times a day.*

BEING IN YOUR FEMININE ENERGY

The following segment has to do with the principles of tantra. This subject is a bit complicated, but there are numerous books written on the subject if you are interested. *What does it mean to be feminine?* This doesn't mean that you need to do what women are expected to do or that you even must be female bodied. When discussing feminine energy, it means identifying and distinguishing the difference between your masculine and feminine energy and using your feminine energy more within the context of relationships. Everyone has both masculine and feminine energies in their body. A lot of things we do within our culture activate that masculine energy. Examples of masculine energy include striving to be in control, pushing to get more done, and competing with others. Your feminine energy is about receiving, accepting, creating, being sensual, exploring, openness, intuitiveness, and, ultimately, about loving.

Once we learn how to accept our bodies, how to find our feminine energy, and how to quiet the negative worries in our minds, we are well on our way to having a great sexual life. These qualities of self-love, confidence, loving energy, and reduced anxiety help us talk to our partners about what we desire sexually. If you are not able to talk about desires with your sexual partner, then there is a chance your sex life will be less than ideal.

How and When to Talk to Your Partner About Sex

There is no magic way to become comfortable with discussing sex with your partner or to make your partner feel entirely comfortable discussing sex with you. The only way is to start talking, acknowledge that it may be uncomfortable/hard/strange to talk about, and then continue talking. One partner may be more willing to engage in conversations around sex than the other, which is perfectly okay. It is important to respect where you are as well as where your partner is in terms of comfort level.

There are ways to address each other in the moment. If your partner is not hitting the right spot on your clit or is missing your clit entirely, you can say things like, "Up a little" or "To the right a little." You can adjust your body so you are in the right position. Partners, please note that if a woman adjusts her body while you are touching her, do not move your hand or mouth. Unless she is moaning and kicking you, she is probably not squirming with pleasure. She may be trying to readjust to get in a more pleasurable position. When your partner does hit the right spot, provide positive reinforcement, like, "Oh, that is it"; "It feels so good. Stay right there"; "Yes, yes, please don't move"; or "You are awesome. Keep doing that."

Some issues that come up during sex could be chronic problems. However, addressing them in the moment does not help. In this case it is good to discuss the subject outside the bedroom when you are both calm and have time to engage properly. As you are rushing out the door in the morning or getting ready to go to sleep is not a great time to begin a conversation around your sexual pleasure. Perhaps when you are lying around watching television or cleaning up the dishes after dinner might be the right time to broach the subject. Pick the right moment. Ask your partner if he or she has fifteen minutes because you want to talk about something. If your partner says yes, then you can bring it up at that time. If your partner says he or she is busy, ask for a time that would work better. Avoid ending the conversation until the other person can agree on a time to chat with you.

Example: Sandy has been experiencing pain when having sex with her partner because she is not fully aroused when he penetrates her.

Communicating during a Sexual Encounter:

The wrong way: "Stop. You always try to have sex with me too quickly."

The right way: "It would be so hot if you touched me gently right now. I like when you tease me a little bit more before you touch my clit."

Communicating outside of a Sexual Encounter:

The wrong way: "It hurts when you have sex with me."

The right way: "Our sex is great, but sometimes it hurts and makes me feel uncomfortable. Can we add a little more foreplay before we have sex? I would love it if you would give me a massage before you penetrate me."

Imagine that your partner is addressing a problem with you in the "wrong" way. How does each interaction leave you feeling? I suggest that when communicating with you partner, you state what the concern is, explain how it makes you feel, and then offer a suggestion for how to make it better. Doing this will empower your partner; it allows the other person to know what is going on with you and how your partner can help resolve the issue. It is important to discuss sex frequently, as it is much easier to discuss any issues if the lines of communication are already open. Even more important is that many issues around sex can transform into a more serious issue if you do not talk about sex regularly.

CONCLUSIONS

Chapter 1 was written to help you understand the importance of being your authentic self, to understand the use of feminine energy, to help ease some of your anxieties around sexuality and talking about sexuality, and to help empower you in the body you have been given. The duration of the book is more of a how-to guide to use as a resource manual for you and your sexual partner. Through trial and error with your partner, and by picking up new techniques and methods, you will weave your way to a new, amazing sex life.

CHAPTER 2

ANATOMY AND THE BODY

To ACHIEVE GREAT sexual experiences, it is important to understand your anatomy. Feel free to take a mirror and look at your genitals if you never have before.

WOMEN'S BODIES

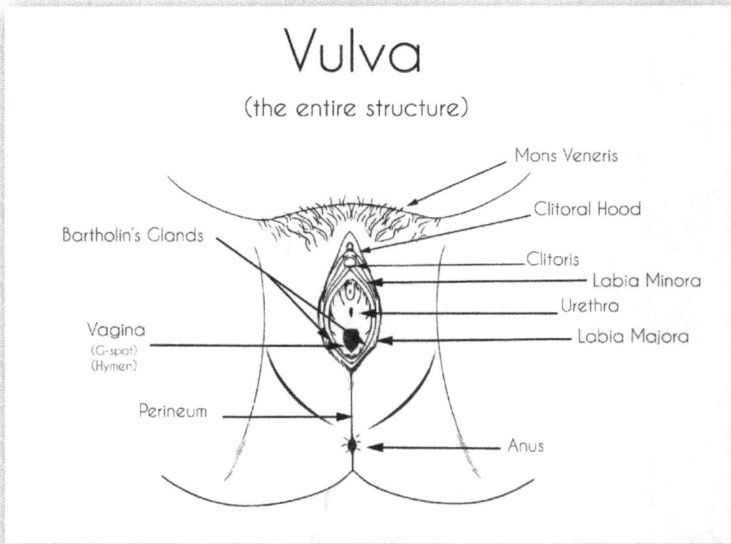

The vulva: This is what you see when you look down. It is commonly referred to as the vagina, but this is incorrect. The vulva is the external part of the female genitals. Where the pubic hair grows on top is called the mons veneris (meaning "hill of Venus," the Roman goddess of love). It protects the pubic bone from the impact of sexual intercourse. This is the fatty tissue of the vulva that you may choose to shave or wax (which will be discussed further in the section on prepping your body for pleasure).

Vaginal lips: The outer lips (labia majora) are covered in hair. Pulling these outer lips open, you will expose the inner labia (labia minora). These do not have any hair on them. All women's lips have different colors, sizes, and shapes. The inner lips are there to protect the clitoris, urethra, and the vagina. Usually the lips (both inner and outer) are sensitive to touch.

The clitoris (clit): The clitoris is the only organ in the body whose sole function is for pleasure. The clitoris looks like a small button right at the top of the outer lips. There is a piece of skin, just inside the inner labia, known as the clitoral hood. This protects the clit from getting too much direct stimulation. The clitoris is the most excitable part of the female genitalia because this is where most pleasurable sensation comes from. There are more nerve endings in the clitoris than in the head of a man's penis, which makes the clit extremely sensitive to touch and stimulation.

The clitoris goes deep inside the body as well (the internal clitoris). When we are embryos in the womb, males and females have the same sexual organs for the first eight weeks of development.[1] The erectile tissue that becomes the penis in males is the tissue that forms the clitoris in women. Although you can only see a small gland of the clitoris externally, the clitoris is about four inches long inside of the body. There are legs that stretch down on both sides of the vagina and bulbs next to those legs that fill up with blood when aroused. Some research says that eight percent of women can orgasm from intercourse alone while the others require clitoral stimulation to orgasm.[2] This statistic comes from

---

1 Chalker, Rebecca. *The Clitoral Truth*. New York: Seven Stories Press, 2000.
2 Wallen, Kim, and Elisabeth A. Lloyd. "Female sexual arousal: Genital anatomy and orgasm in intercourse." *Hormones and Behavior* 59 (2011): 780-792.

a comprehensive analysis of thirty-three studies over the past eighty years by Elisabeth Lloyd.

The urethra: About an inch to two below the clitoris is a teeny, tiny hole that you may not even be able to see clearly. This is where you pee from and where female ejaculate comes from.[3] You will learn more about female ejaculation (also known as "squirting") later in the book.

The vagina: Under the urethra is a bigger hole, which is your vagina. You do not pee from your vagina, but it is where you are penetrated during digital (fingering) or penetrative intercourse. It is where blood comes from during your period, and it is the birth canal. The vagina has most of its nerve endings in the first third of the opening. The reason for this is evolutionary—if the entire vagina had numerous nerve endings, it would be extremely painful to give birth to a baby through the vaginal canal. The surprising lack of nerve endings in the vagina is what accounts for the difficulty many women have in achieving orgasm through vaginal penetration alone. Remember how we discussed the clitoris and how it is also inside the body? Vaginal orgasms stem from stimulation of the internal clitoris. Most women need direct stimulation of the external clitoris also. Therefore, you should not feel bad or inadequate if vaginal penetration alone does not do it for you. Feel free to explain this to your partner if he expresses the desire to give you an orgasm through vaginal penetration alone.

Bartholin's glands: These glands are the first step in lubrication. It is kind of like precome (male ejaculate) for women. These two small glands are near the bottom of the vulva with openings on either side of the vagina. They are located underneath the skin, and they provide a small amount of lubricant.

The G-spot: It is more of an area than a spot. Some state that you can locate the G-spot by inserting your fingers into your vagina and

---

3 Schubach, Gary. "Urethral Expulsions During Sexual Arousal and Bladder Catheterization in Seven Human Females." *Electronic Journal of Human Sexuality* 4 (2001).

making the "come here" motion. When a woman is aroused, this area can get harder, and the texture can change. Some believe that the G-spot is the internal bulbs of the clitoris, located behind the left and right walls of the vagina. Therefore, the G-spot is the whole area of the internal clitoris. Stimulating this at the same time as the external clitoris can create tons of pleasure for women. When your G-spot is stimulated, it can make you feel as though you should pee, but you won't. If any liquid comes out, it may be female ejaculate, otherwise known as squirting. It feels this way because the inner clitoris is enlarged when stimulated, which can put pressure on your bladder. Knowing how to engage this area of your body can lead to great pleasure and multiple orgasms.

The hymen: A piece of tissue that lines the vaginal opening. It is the "cherry" that is referred to in the common "popped her cherry" quote. Unlike the saying goes, the hymen has no barometer on whether or not the woman is a virgin. This tissue can be stretched with a finger, tampon, or anything inserted into the vagina. Sometimes this wears away naturally, and sometimes it remains so thick that it makes first penetration extremely painful. If intercourse continues to be painful after you have been penetrated, there is a chance that this barrier has not been broken, and you can see a gynecologist, who can help with this.

The perineum: The piece of skin from the bottom of the vulva to the anus is called the perineum. There are not many nerve endings here for women, and sometimes doctors cut through this to open the canal for women who have vaginal births.

The anus: Believe it or not, it has numerous sensitive nerve endings. Many people practice anal sex, and it is important to note that the anus also has the capacity to be penetrated as the vagina does. The only difference is that the anus does not self-lubricate, as does the vagina. Therefore when engaging in anal sex, make sure to use a lot of lube. In 2005 a Centers for Disease Control and Prevention (CDC) survey found that 40 percent of females ages twenty-four to forty-four engaged in anal sex.

Try This Out

Educate your partner on the size of the clitoris using what you have just read. Some things to ask yourself:

- *Have you ever had anal sex? Is that something you would want to try?*
- *Have you ever had a G-spot orgasm or given someone a G-spot orgasm?*

Pleasure during Your Period

Many women still want to have sex when they are on their period and want to know if it is safe. Having intercourse while on your period is safe and can, in fact, help with cramps and relieve body tension. Societal norms tend to put a certain level of shame on women, telling them to be clean and discreet when they are on their period. The truth is that women still experience pleasure when they are on their periods, so period sex should not be ruled out. Per one man interviewed, "When [period sex] is happening, it is fine, but the aftereffect can be somewhat shocking." Therefore, before engaging in period sex, it is important to make sure both parties agree.

You should be aware of some things when having period sex. You can still get pregnant, so please use a form of birth control. Another concern is the location of your cervix. During this time of the month, the cervix is slightly lower, so if your partner is penetrating you deeply, it may hurt more. The walls of the vagina may also feel more sensitive. Be sure to communicate this to your partner if you experience any discomfort.

The first time you try period sex, stick to one of your lighter days. For example, if day one and two are particularly heavy, wait until days three through five. This way you won't have to stress about the blood, and you can assess how your body responds to intercourse during your period. Put down a dark-colored towel on top of the sheets so that all the fluid will be absorbed. Keep some tissues or paper towels handy so that you can wipe off when you're done before you stand up. Try the missionary position, as it is the position where you will have the least amount of blood leaving the vagina. Also note that using lube over a condom will help with the dryness that can occur from tampon-use during periods.

TRY THIS OUT

Ask your partner:

- *"Have you ever had sex while on your period or with someone who was on their period?"*
- *"Have you ever had a bad experience with periods that turned you off from it?"*

PREPPING THE BODY FOR PLEASURE
WEIGHT

You can't go anywhere without seeing an advertisement with a thin model and thinking, "Man, if only my body looked like that…" Well, I am here to tell you that most people do not look like that, and even if you did, you would find something else that you thought was wrong with you. Most people, no matter what weight or body shape, have a part of them that they would want to work on or could use some improvement. The trick to maintaining weight is eating healthy and balanced meals. Health is much more important than weight, and the goal is to be a physically healthy person. It is important to love your body. A lot of times, I see people saying women should "love their bodies" while they eat junk food all day. I think it is important to note that loving our bodies means taking care of our bodies and not eating junk food regularly. Our bodies need healthy foods, even if our minds crave junk food. So try to remember to love your body with some extra fruits and vegetables.

After health comes confidence. No matter what your body structure, it is important that you love you. If you do, others will too. If you constantly hate how you look, you will attract people who give you the same feedback. Realize your worth. How do you become confident with your body? Again, positive affirmations! When you look at yourself in the mirror, let yourself admire your body or at least pretend to. What would you say to your best friend? Say those kind things to yourself. It is okay if you don't believe it yet. Just say it and focus on being positive toward yourself. Find at least one thing to say each day. Focus on this instead of the problem areas that you have identified.

PHEROMONES

Sometimes people believe it is best to shower, use scented soaps, spray their hair and bodies with perfume, and douse their clothes in detergents. However, as you do this, you can be taking away from your pheromones. These are the natural smells our bodies emit to attract people to us. The idea of perfume and scented soaps came about to enhance smell, yet people go overboard. You can be right next to someone and not even smell any part of the other person's body. Scent is one of the most important aspects of attraction. Alongside sight and being physically attracted to someone, the way your body responds to how a person smells will correlate to whether you are attracted to this person. In some cases someone's scent will repel another person. This is usually a physiological response that occurs due to immune systems not matching up for reproductive purposes. When everyone is covered in perfume and cologne, it makes it hard to distinguish our actual physiological attraction. Therefore, lay off the perfume, buy scent-free detergent, and let your body attract the right match.

PUBIC HAIR

People often wonder what to do with their pubic hair. There are a variety of preferences for pubic hair, and the latest trend of little to no pubic hair seems to be influenced by the current porn industry, which often shows women completely waxed. It is important to be aware that pubic hair is subject to the same standards of beauty that the rest of women's bodies are subjected to. Twenty years ago, women were not hairless in the way that they are now. The question of hair or no hair is not a simple one and does not have a simple answer. Some women choose to leave their pubic hair because they like the look or to protest the idea that women's vulvas should be hairless. Some women choose to leave their pubic hair as is because they do not want to put the time or energy into grooming. Some women go hairless because it is what their partner prefers. Some go hairless because it is what they prefer. And some women go hairless because they think they should. Going hairless can mean different things to different people. For some it means absolutely no hair; for others it means having a "landing strip," a small patch of pubic hair on the vulva. The important thing to remember when deciding what to do with your pubic hair is that you are comfortable with what you have. The next important person to consult is your partner. It may be good to get your partner's opinion since every partner is different and there is not one pubic hair look that is appreciated by all.

If you do decide to go hairless or remove some of your pubic hair, you have a few options to remove it. The main methods are bikini waxing, Brazilian waxing, shaving, chemical hair removal (e.g., Nair), laser hair removal, and electrolysis. A good in-between method is trimming your pubic hair with an electric razor that is specifically designed for women. If you want the hair totally gone, here are some of the common methods.

Bikini waxing: Bikini waxing is less invasive than Brazilian waxing, but it can still be very painful. Typically bikini waxes remove the hair around the vulva.
Approximate cost: twenty-five to forty-five dollars.

Brazilian waxing: With Brazilian waxing, most, if not all, of the hair is removed from all over (your vulva, outer labia, and anus). It is painful, but the result is nice because you do not even have to think about pubic hair for a few weeks. You might be sensitive all over for a few days while your skin adjusts to not having hair as protection, but generally, that discomfort subsides and you adjust to being hairless. To be consistent you should wax every three to four weeks, which can get expensive. It is important not to shave in between waxing though because it interferes with hair growth and can lead to a more painful waxing experience. Approximate cost: fifty to seventy dollars (there are drugstore-brand waxes that take some practice, but make it much less expensive).

Shaving: Some say shaving is the easiest form of getting rid of hair. However, it can cause problems such as razor burn and bumps. First of all use a nice razer. Be sure to use a scent-free shaving cream and all-natural balm afterward to eliminate any irritation and redness. The last place you want to have a bad reaction is on the sensitive skin of the vulva.
Approximate cost: five to fifteen dollars.

Chemical hair removal: Nair can work as it has depilatories which chemically dissolves the hair on contact. It does have a strong odor to it.
Approximate cost: six to twelve dollars.

Laser hair removal/electrolysis: If you want permanent hair removal, this is your best option. Although expensive and time consuming, after about ten sessions, you will notice less and thinner hair in this area. It cuts down on grooming time in the future and leaves less work if any hair does last through the treatments. A word of caution: hair that has been removed by laser hair removal can grow back when you are pregnant due to a change in hormones. This means that it could require more costly and painful treatments. It has also been the case for some people that it does not work at all.
Approximate cost: more than $800.

MALE BODIES

In the United States, there is a tendency to put a good deal of emphasis on penis size. In popular media the question is often "How big is he?"

which implies the underlying notion that being bigger is better. But bigger is not always better. My opinion on penis size is that it is your relationship with the penis that matters.

Big penises are like big houses. Aesthetically a big penis looks great on the outside, much like a big house. Just like big houses are harder to clean and cost more to maintain, big penises can be harder to perform oral sex on and can cause pain during penetration because they can hit the cervix or stretch the vaginal opening more than what is comfortable. With a smaller penis, there may not be any pain, yet some women state that they experience less physical pleasure.

Regardless of the penis size, the pleasure women will derive from a man's penis is more correlated to how much she likes that penis and the technique that the penis is using. Just like other aspects of physical attraction, we get attracted to a penis. It is perfectly normal for a woman not to be attracted to a penis at first and then grow to appreciate it. The emotional and mental attachment you get to the penis contributes to your pleasure.

I could go into what the average penis size is, but that is only feeding into the misconstrued idea that there are size parameters that are okay or standard sizes that are acceptable, which is not accurate. If you partner's penis gives you pleasure, it is the perfect size regardless of how big or small it is. If you partner's penis is not giving you pleasure, it may be the way your partner is using his penis. If so, now would be a good time to explore new positions and techniques.

CIRCUMCISION

It is currently debated in this country whether a man should have a circumcised penis or not. The popular narrative seems to elevate circumcised penises as better or more desirable. I know many women who have stated that noncircumcised penises have led to more pleasure for her and for her partner because noncircumcised penises are more lubricating than circumcised ones. Some women prefer the look of a circumcised penis, while others do not notice much of a difference. There is nothing to be scared of if you encounter a noncircumcised penis. They just have some extra skin, the foreskin, which covers the head of the penis while flaccid and retracts back when the penis is erect.

ERECTIONS

If you are in a sexual space with a male partner and he is not hard, that is totally normal. Pornography depicts men as always ready to go. They see a naked woman and are hard almost immediately. Life is not like that. If you see that your partner's penis is soft, but he is in the moment with you and giving other signs that he is into the sexual act and enjoying himself, I encourage you to let go of the notion that it should be hard and continue to enjoy each other sexually. A soft penis is not an automatic indication that your partner is not into the sexual experience. Soft penises are an indication that blood has not yet entered the penis. Getting upset about a physiological response that he may not have control over ruins the moment more than a soft penis does. Do not put pressure on this unless it becomes a constant problem that he can never get an erection while with you. If this is the case, it may be time to discuss what is happening and consult a physician or sex therapist.

DIFFERENCE BETWEEN ORGASMING AND EJACULATING

I have heard people state that it is easy to tell when men have orgasmed because they ejaculated. Although most men orgasm and ejaculate at the same time, this is not always the case. Through sacred sexuality practices, I know that there is a difference between orgasming and ejaculation. Ejaculation is the fluid that is dispelled from the body. Orgasm can be the emotional, mental, and physical part of this process. People can achieve full-body orgasms using breath-work and relaxation of the mind and body. Sometimes an ejaculatory and full-body orgasm can occur together, and other times, the male body can orgasm without the penis ejaculating at all.

CONCLUSIONS

It is important to understand your anatomy as a female and information about your partner's body. Feel free to talk with your friends and sexual partner about your body. Instead of shaming the body, as many are taught to do while growing up, praise it as well as the body of your sexual partner. If you feel attracted to your partner, make sure to say which exact parts you value. Doing this will also set up the framework for you to appreciate your body.

CHAPTER 3

SEX TALK

SEX, DRUGS, AND ALCOHOL

No MATTER WHAT you have heard, combining sex with drugs and/or alcohol is a bad idea. It takes away your ability to be close to your partner and make clear, conscious decisions about the encounter you want to have.

I hear people say, "Have a drink or two at the start of your date. It'll loosen you up." My thought is that you should be able to hang out with someone without alcohol. If this person is going to become a partner, the two of you will have to hang out sober at some point. Starting out as your authentic, sober self is ideal.

No matter how many times people will say, "Drunk sex is great," it is not. Sex while drinking inhibits your ability to make clear decisions about your boundaries and desires. My suggestion is to have sober sex with your partner.

MASTURBATION

There is a discrepancy between male masturbation and female masturbation. While boys are taught about masturbation during the school "sex talk," girls are taught about periods. What I have seen is that most women discover masturbation on their own and then are shamed because no one teaches them that it is a normal part of sexual development. I have noticed that many women have their first sexual experience with a partner while most men have their first sexual experience with themselves. This can be problematic because women enter sexual relationships without knowing what gives them pleasure. When women do not know what actually brings them sexual pleasure, it impacts their sexual experiences because they are unable to communicate desires to their partners and do not have the language to take control of their pleasure. It is common for females who have never masturbated to be in a sexual relationship and not even know if they have experienced an orgasm.

Many factors can lead to women not masturbating. Some women are not because they do not want to or because society does not give them permission to masturbate in the way that it gives men permission to. Females do not openly talk about masturbation in the way that men do, or if they do, others may view or judge them as promiscuous. Women also might be reluctant because they are not quite sure how to masturbate or they tried one way of masturbating and did not like it. The first thing I believe they should do is get a mirror and look at themselves so they can know their anatomy and see what they are doing while masturbating. In this section I hope to normalize female masturbation and provide helpful information on how to masturbate pleasurably.

You can masturbate alone or with a partner. Masturbating in front of your partner can provide an opportunity for you to show your partner what you enjoy in a fun, sexy way. It is common for people to continue to masturbate alone when they are in a satisfying sexual relationship. It is also common for partners to get upset if they discover that their partner is masturbating. This discovery can cause an individual to wonder whether he or she is satisfying the partner because the other person chooses to masturbate. In my experience if your partner is masturbating for the enjoyment of self-pleasure in addition to your sexual relationship, it is not beneficial to demand that the partner stop masturbating due to your insecurity. Doing this can create problems because you are taking away the other person's pleasure and because the act of masturbating regularly does not take away from a sexual relationship. A person who masturbates usually can achieve more orgasms and more intensity in the pleasure of the orgasms than a person who does not masturbate.

Female masturbation techniques: There are two main spots to utilize when masturbating. One is external, the clitoris, and the other is internal, the vagina and, potentially, the G-spot. Some women enjoy masturbating with their fingers while some women enjoy using toys. Either way can work, and it is worth exploring both avenues, as they both have different effects.

Fingers: Make sure you have time to explore your body. If you are going to use fingers to masturbate for the first time, it may take about a half hour or more to experience pleasure. Lay down in a comfortable position. Touch your body along your neck, over your chest, across your stomach, and down to your vulva. Starting with a light pressure and lube on your index and/or middle finger, rub the clitoris (see anatomy section if needed) in a circular motion. Increase pressure as the clitoris becomes more prominent and firm. You can move your fingers up and down the inner labia or left and right over the vulva. Explore the vaginal opening with your fingers and see if this brings increased pleasure. Use a circular motion in the vaginal opening to prep before inserting fingers inside. Feel around the walls of the vagina and see if any of them feel more pleasurable than others. Some women say the upper wall of the vagina feels best to them, while others would agree that pressure between the left and right walls adds additional stimulation. If you need to bring your other hand down to massage the clitoris while one hand is focused on the vagina, perineum, or anus, do so. Make sure that if you incorporate the anus into masturbation, that you do not use those same fingers in the vagina or on the vulva.

The main point in using your hands and fingers in masturbation is to explore with different locations, degrees of pressure, and strokes. If you don't like the feeling when you use your fingers, remember that this does not necessarily mean you do not like masturbating. It may simply mean that you prefer masturbating with the use of external objects, such as rubbing your genitals on objects that feel pleasurable or using sex toys.

Sex Toys

Many toys are inexpensive and can be easily purchased online. Toys usually get the job done and can lead to orgasms more quickly than using your hands alone. A variety of toys are available, and I will break some of them down for you below.

Bullets: The job of the bullet is to add increased pleasure on the clitoris. If you have never bought a toy before, this is a great place to start. It packs a lot of power into one condensed spot and jolts the nerve endings in the clitoris. Adding a bullet to masturbation and intercourse can greatly increase the intensity and amount of orgasms that you experience. Please note that bullets are external toys and not to be used inside the vagina.

G-spot toys: G-spot toys are made for the vagina. They usually have a curve in them that angles upward to hit what is known as the G-spot. Some women experience additional pleasure with this type of toy because they can turn it and hit the wall of the vagina that they feel is most sensitive.

Dual-action vibrators: The famous "rabbit" toy is a dual-action vibrator. It has one spot that is designated to stimulate the clitoris and a shaft that is made to fill the vagina. If you have never masturbated with a toy before or never had an orgasm, I would not recommend this type as a first toy. Make sure that you buy a dual-action vibrator in which you can control the speed and intensity of the two parts separately so you can control the pleasure.

Dildos: A hard shaft, best when made of silicone, glass, or other solid material, gives the feeling of having a penis inside the vagina. Many women use dildos accompanied by their fingers or a bullet on the clitoris.

TRY THIS OUT

1. *Set one sex-date for yourself each week where you have thirty minutes of alone time to explore what type of touch feels best for your body.*
2. *Purchase an inexpensive sex toy to see how your body responds to a different type of sensation.*

Sex Toys While Having Intercourse

Incorporating sex toys while being with a partner can be an intimidating discussion. However, once you bring it up, excitement can grow, and new types of pleasure may be possible. Do not be shy to bring this topic up with a regular sexual partner if it will help the sexual experience. The goal is to be comfortable with asking for what you need. You can explain to the partner that this does not take away from the connection between the two of you; it simply adds additional stimulation that your body desires.

Orgasming during Intercourse

A lot of pressure exists around men and women to both have orgasms during sex and to have orgasms at the same time. It is often painted as the most successful version of intercourse. Rarely will dual orgasms happen through vaginal stimulation alone. This is true because most women need clitoral stimulation to orgasm, based on how bodies are designed, and intercourse alone does not adequately provide this. It is important to understand this about our bodies and communicate it to our partners. Many women stimulate themselves during intercourse with a partner because they know what feels good in the moment. This is also a great place to incorporate toys. Just play around with it and do what feels good for you without putting pressure on the situation.

Try This Out

Ask your partner:

- *"Did you have the "sex talk" in middle school? What did you learn?"*
- *"Can we try an encounter where we both masturbate in front of one another?"*
- *"What are your thoughts on sex toys?"*

THE MADONNA AND THE WHORE

Everyone has an opinion on when women should be having sex. The message to men tends to be, "The sooner, the better." The message to women is "If you have sex you are a slut," and "If you wait, you are a prude." Religion tells us to wait until marriage, media tells us to go for it, and our peers hold mixed judgment. In the end there is no right answer of when to have sex.

If you end up having sex with the "wrong person" at first, it is okay. If you have sex with multiple people before the age of twenty, it is okay. The most harmful thing people can do is become more focused on the number of sexual partners versus the quality of the partners, the lessons learned from relationships or sexual encounters, and what they teach them about themselves.

Because women are often shamed for having "too many" sexual partners, another message has emerged: fun, sexy, empowered, power-ful women have as much sex as they want, with as many partners as they want, and with as little emotion involved as they want. Having as much sex as you want can be great, but it is important to make sure that you are choosing to have sexual encounters based on what you truly want, not because others may perceive doing it as fun or sexy. A trend is developing where women are emotionally distancing themselves from relationships and vulnerability by focusing on the physical aspects as opposed to the emotions. This is the exact opposite of what I believe should be happening within women's sexual lives. Intercourse with an-other person is a great opportunity for connection and intimacy while incorporating physical pleasure. There is a chance that having sex with multiple people who you do not wish to be connected to can harm your ability to be vulnerable to others, thus making it more difficult when you start having sex with someone with whom you want to form an inti-mate bond.

Our sexuality and sexual experiences are not stagnant moments that live in our memories. They are evolving pieces of ourselves that we con-tinually redefine. What happened in the past does not have to be what happens in the future! If in the past you have slept with partners and regretted it, try taking more time to get to know partners before sleeping with them in the future. If you feel that you have missed out because you have not had sexual experiences with partners and you wish you had, allow yourself to be open to the sexual experiences you wish to have in the future. Remember that you must make different choices to get different results. It is incredibly powerful when you chose to be in control of your sexual experiences from a perspective of recognizing your value and taking charge of who enters your life and your body and when and how that happens. When you have a perspective of "I am worth it" versus looking to others to confirm your worth, you will make the best, healthiest choices for yourself. Do what feels right for you, and let go of what others think while avoiding the limitations and boundaries people will try to place on you.

What I Wish I Knew My First Time

I sent the following message to my friends:

> *Hi! I'm working on a book about sex and want to put a section in it called "What I wish I knew my first time." Do you have any sage pieces of advice you could tell to the new generation?*

Below are their responses.

I will tell you what I've seen from working with thirteen- to twenty-five-year-olds:

1. Regret over not getting tested. Typically one partner has had sex, and the person who is having sex for the first time ends up with a sexually transmitted infection (STI).

PLAYTIME: NOT JUST FOR CHILDREN

2. Not using a condom. Most want their first time to be special, and it almost seems like a condom will ruin the bond or that special time. Then the girl ends up at the clinic worrying about pregnancy and STIs.

3. Waiting. An overwhelming amount of patients always wish they would have waited longer to have sex and to get to know the person. Especially when they end up with an STI and are heartbroken because they thought their partner was being faithful.

4. Knowledge. It always amazes me how little thirteen- to twenty-five-year-olds actually know about STIs and its transmission. Some use condoms for vaginal or anal sex but not for oral sex. By the same token, a lot of my clients have anal sex to prevent pregnancy, preserve "virginity," and don't use condoms because they feel condoms are to prevent pregnancy only. Most don't know how to put one on properly and don't follow instructions with birth control and back-up methods. In general most are clueless about STIs.

Some helpful advice:

• Health: Address health risks before exposing yourself to them. Don't wait until afterward.
• Partnership: Have sex with people who you can be friends with, people you feel comfortable hanging out with while you're both sober (drinking buddies don't count). Also make sure you're both on the same page about what kind of partnership you're looking for—casual, exclusive, etc.
• Explore and enjoy!

It's not anywhere near as sexy as you were led to believe. It can be awkward, uncomfortable, and messy. But also fun, funny, romantic, and heartfelt. And if you don't feel comfortable being a little bit embarrassed and exploring these things with your partner, then think again about what you're about to do and who with! If you can't laugh with the person about the reality of the situation, then you may be experiencing pressure to keep up appearances or pull it off flawlessly, which will only detract from this moment in your life. It's an exploration…let yourself enjoy it with someone you don't need to impress, and try to give yourself a reality check beforehand so that you don't go into it expecting a Hollywood version of sex. Prepare for the *National Geographic* version; you'll have a much better time!

Women, if you're afraid of your partner seeing a hair out of place or a hair, period…*proceed with caution*! Your body is a natural creation with its own needs and agenda. It will do things you didn't expect and cannot control. Not that you need to sport a wild bush (whatever kind of grooming you choose to do or not is up to you!), but your nerves about appearances can be a great measuring stick in letting you know how prepared and comfortable you might be for the things to come. I don't want this to scare you…sex isn't a fart fest with liquids shooting all over the place! But it can happen! It does happen. And if it does, it's never awesome, but it shouldn't be devastating either. Again if you can't laugh about it, try to learn how!

My high school boyfriend and I were both virgins and both terrified of becoming pregnant. We fooled around a lot, and I am so thankful for that period of my life. Kissing can be awesome when it's the only thing you've ever done. And those kisses meant everything because we were fully present, not just racing past it onto something else. And when you move on to the next level of intimacy, that level is incredible because it's the furthest you've ever gone. It's new territory. Once we had sex, years later, we never spent that same amount of time being with each other in those other ways. There was always this goal of sex to arrive at or achieve. The playground of foreplay was wonderful in those years because there was a freedom to hang out there a while. We weren't distracted by this urgency to get to the big bang. It was some of the most intimate moments I've had in my sexual life to date.

⁓

My only piece of advice is to be aware of the bond that it creates. Somehow you look at that person differently and may miss quite a few warning signs because of the bond. It's not just some lame thing that people tell you to scare you—it's true.

⁓

Make sure you are worth it before you think he is worth it.

SEXUAL DESIRE

The topic of when to have sex and how much to have sex can trigger shame in some women. As women we often feel shame around the way our bodies are shaped, the ways we experience pleasure, and if we choose to engage or abstain sexually. The broad expectation pop culture perpetuates is for women to act sexually in response to a man's sexual drive. Woman's pleasure is often portrayed as dependent on a man and is born out of a response to a man's arousal. This expectation does not consider a broad number of factors.

Sexual drive and desire are not things you either have or don't have. Varying degrees of these elements are present. They change from person to person and can change from day to day or minute to minute. Having a different level of desire than your partner is completely normal. While every partner is not going to be satisfied every minute, overall the goal is to find equilibrium where both partners are satisfied. You can achieve this state in several ways. The first step is good communication. You need to communicate to your partner when you are aroused and when you are not so your partner can learn the difference. It is not doing you or the other person any favors to pretend to be aroused when you are not. It sets up a pattern of unsatisfying sexual encounters.

Mismatched libidos can be frustrating for both parties. If you are the one wanting to have sex more than your partner, discuss this and figure out a way to meet both your needs. Maybe one night a week, your partner watches you masturbate, another night your partner gets you to orgasm without intercourse, and one night you have penetrative sex. There also does not have to be shame associated with you or your partner masturbating on your own. It is important to let go of the idea that if you or your partner masturbates, it is because you or the other person is not being satisfied. Many people in relationships that are sexually satisfied masturbate. Sexual satisfaction in a relationship directly correlates to knowing your body.

Many women do not want to have sex because it is not pleasurable or it is painful. If you are experiencing painful intercourse, I encourage that you discuss this issue with your doctor. If you do not feel comfortable before or after discussing this with your doctor, I recommend seeking help from an AASECT certified sex therapist. The advantage to seeing a sex therapist is that such a professional can provide you with emotional support and recommend alternative treatment options you may not have considered. A sex therapist can also lead you to a sex-positive doctor; not all doctors are trained in how to value healthy sexuality.

Try This Out

Let your partner know if you are not fully aroused by suggesting an alternative approach:

- *"It is so hot when you touch my neck; can you do that more?"*
- *"Before we have sex, why don't we give each other full-body massages?"*
- *"This is so hot. Can you tease me a little longer? I love this feeling of wanting you."*

RELATIONSHIP FOREPLAY TIPS

When you are in a relationship, it is important to remember a few things prior to the sexual encounter. Within relationships, people sometimes forget the foreplay and excitement aspect and instead fall into a routine. Touching your partner throughout the day to get the other person into a sexual state is important. Don't forget to kiss regularly, as if you were just beginning your dating life together. Try to be flirtatious throughout the day, and offer your partner compliments. If it feels right to you, try to use dirty or sexual talk with your partner. As world-renowned therapist Esther Perel says, foreplay starts the moment after your last orgasm.

ORAL SEX TECHNIQUES

If want to give your partner an awesome oral sex experience, you first must commit to the process and be authentic in your desire to please your partner orally. Sometimes people have had bad experiences with oral sex that prevent them from wanting to give or get oral sex now. So talk to you partner about it and ask if your partner has any issues with giving oral sex. Together come up with ways to make it so both partners are comfortable. Use positive affirmations if you need to, such as "I am great at this." Why? Because if you tell yourself "I am so bad at this; I am doing horribly" or "I hate this; it is gross," that will translate to your partner. Make sure your mind knows that this is what you want to be doing. If you are not in this mind-set, then your oral skills won't be up to par.

The timeline: Some people get overwhelmed by the thought of giving a blowjob or going down on a woman until it is over. Some partners can last thirty minutes, and this thought can stop you from even starting oral sex. But it shouldn't. It is perfectly fine to tell your partner, "I am going down on you to start things off, and then I want penetration." This gives you the power to go down on your partner as long as it is enjoyable for you, and then you can switch to something else.

Before you start, ask if any parts of the body are off-limits. Ask if you have free rein to touch thighs, ass, stomach, etc. before you begin giving a partner oral sex. If you are going down on a man, discuss ejaculation in your mouth prior to oral sex. If you do not want your partner to ejaculate in your mouth, ask him if he would be willing to come elsewhere.

While going down on your partner, make sure you ask what feels good. Get an idea of the pressure that works, the spot that is most sensitive, and what does not feel good. Make sure your body is in a comfortable position. Also be sure that you are not focusing on what you look like and that you are focused on your partner's experience. If you need to move your partner, then do so. If you have long hair, tie it out of your face. Give positive feedback to your partner about how you are enjoying this experience. Communicate and experiment with an open mind.

Some females are concerned with receiving oral sex due to fear about how their vulvas look. If you ever feel that your labia doesn't look normal, I suggest a google search on vaginal lips and look at the variety. If you are concerned about the smell of your vagina, remember that many men enjoy that smell. Ask your partner what his opinion is and if he likes how it looks and how it smells. Validation from your partner is probably more helpful than anything I can tell you. If both of you are concerned with genital odors, try to incorporate a shower as part of the foreplay and aftercare (If there is significant odor, there is a chance that there is bacterial vaginosis and you should make an appointment with your doctor).

If you and your partner have tried some of the tips above and still do not want to engage in oral sex, it is okay. If this is the case, and neither partner is concerned about it, then that can be the end of oral sex for now. But if one partner would like to receive stimulation beyond vaginal intercourse, I encourage you to read the sex toy section and discover if using a toy might help.

LENGTH OF SEX

Some women love having sex that lasts for hours. Some women love intense, short sexual encounters. *Sex and the City* did a good job of highlighting how different women want different things from sex. Some women like to use bondage, toys, and different positions during a sexual episode, and some women like to stay in missionary. We all have different preferences that we must then combine with our partners' preferences to create sexual encounters that are pleasurable for all parties. Do what feels good for you and your partner without worrying what you *should* be doing.

Often a lot of pressure and expectation gets put on the length of sexual intercourse and how long a male partner can maintain an erection. A recent statistic shows that the average length of intercourse is 7.3 minutes.[4] Several factors contribute to how long sex will take. The time in between sexual activity can have an impact either way on length. Some men last longer when they have recently had sex while others will come more quickly. While some men are okay with orgasming multiple times in one day, others require more time to recharge and wish to wait longer between sexual encounters. It is also important to figure out what you prefer and work with your partner to achieve it. For example if you prefer shorter sexual encounters but your partner lasts a long time and has recently ejaculated, it may be better for you to set a guideline against back-to-back sexual encounters. I suggest guidelines instead of rules because they allow for more flexibility.

TOUCHING YOUR PARTNER

The question of touching your partner after a sexual encounter was recently presented to me. A client wanted to know if and how to touch one's partner after the partner has ejaculated. This is dependent on the person. If you have the desire to touch your partner after he has ejaculated, ask first. If you have a desire to be touched or held after orgasming, it would be good to ask your partner before the sexual encounter if he or she is willing to hold you afterward.

---

4 Corty, Eric, and Jenay Guardiani. "Canadian and American Sex Therapists' Perceptions of Normal and Abnormal Ejaculatory Latencies: How Long Should Intercourse Last?" *The Journal of Sexual Medicine* 5 (2005): 1251-1256.

Not in the Mood

What happens when you do not want to have sex? If you do not want to ever have sex again with a partner with whom you have been intimate with before, you have the option of saying a permanent no to having sex. If you do not want to have sex with a partner in the moment because you are feeling unloved or hurt, it is important to address this with the other person.

I do not advocate forcing yourself to have sex when you are not in the mood, but I do suggest that you ground yourself in your five senses before pushing your partner away. No one likes being rejected with little explanation, so I encourage you to try an alternate approach. If you do not want to have sex because you are tired, you could lovingly suggest another time. Sex dates are an excellent idea if you are having difficulty finding time to connect with your partner sexually. I suggest it to clients all the time! I know it may sound weird, but when you first got together with your partner and you did not live together, it created anticipation looking forward to a date night, knowing that you would see each other and have sex.

Conclusions

From masturbation, to partner sex, to foreplay, to libidos, there are numerous things to consider within a sexual encounter. Make sure that you take the time to learn your sexual preferences alone and with your sexual partner. Knowing your body is an important part of being able to agree to partnered sex.

CHAPTER 4

Know Your Worth

Cheating

"Texting another person is cheating!"
"Porn is cheating!"
"Strip clubs are cheating!"
"Kissing…kissing is definitely cheating!"

IN MY PRACTICE, all of these have been considered cheating by one partner. Yet a fact that may blow your mind is that in some relationships, none of these would be considered cheating! If you are in a relationship with one or multiple people, such as polyamory, swinging, or an open relationship, make sure you clearly define what you view as cheating behaviors. All individuals need to discuss cheating boundaries among themselves; no one can simply assume what the cheating guidelines are.

Let each partner you have know what your limits are on certain behaviors with others. Not everyone has the same idea of what behaviors count as cheating, so you cannot assume. Discuss this openly, and be flexible with the gray areas. For example maybe you can compromise that texting another person isn't cheating, yet if one party sends naked photos, then a boundary has been violated.

Boundaries—For the First Time and *Every* Time

Ladies, use your words when discussing boundaries and desires. Do not assume that the person you hook up with or are in a relationship with knows exactly what you like. Be specific with your partner if you like sex rough or gentle, what forms of stimulation feel good to you, and what parts of your body are sensitive to touch in a pleasurable way or too sensitive to be touched at all. Every person is different and likes to be pleasured in a special way. Make sure you share this with your partner.

Similarly if you do not want a certain sexual activity done to you, make sure you know how to express that clearly. It can make your partner more nervous to have free rein over your body than it does to have guidelines about what you enjoy. Just because you have agreed and want to have sex or date someone does not mean that you no longer have boundaries. You still have the ultimate say over what happens to your body, and I encourage you to communicate those boundaries and leave any situation in which you are not being listened to.

When Boundaries Are Violated

A shocking number of women in this country have reported being sexually assaulted. I suspect that even more women have experienced sexual assault and not reported it or labeled it as such. When women are young, they are told to be careful of the stranger lurking in the bushes; in fact many sexual assault perpetrators are friends or family. It can be a confusing situation because, yes, your boundaries were violated, but you feel some responsibility because you "asked for it" by drinking too much, or your boyfriend "just got carried away," or you were young and curious, or you felt like you didn't say no forcefully enough. In these situations it is important to remember that it is not your fault and that your boundaries were violated. It is also important to note that you are still 100 percent able to have and enjoy a sex life.

For some people, if sexual assault has taken place, it is helpful to talk to a therapist or counselor about what happened. Some people find it helpful to talk to their friends about it, and others do not want to talk about it at all. There is no right way to go about it. But I encourage you to feel unashamed about what happened and to get the support you need so you can have the great sex life you deserve. Just because something bad happened to you does not mean that you are bad, broken, or damaged. It means nothing about you. The fact that you are still okay despite something bad happening to you means that you are strong and resilient. If you are in a situation where your boundaries are still being violated, I encourage you to get help to leave that situation.

Safe Sex

When you choose to have sex with someone, it is incredibly important to do so safely. By having sexual experiences, you put yourself at risk. However, by being informed about health and protection, you lower the chances of that risk.

Carry Condoms

As women sometimes it feels awkward and uncomfortable to carry condoms. You may be opposed to carrying condoms because you believe that others will perceive you to be slutty or promiscuous because you have protection. You may not carry condoms because you thought that was your partner's job. Just like women take birth control or use intrauterine devices (IUDs), carrying condoms is just another safe way to help manage the risk of sexually transmitted infections (STIs) and pregnancy. Having condoms available is a positive way to take your sexuality into your own hands and not rely on someone else. In my experience I have never heard of a male who did not want to sleep with a female because she had condoms.

Condom Tips

1. Carry condoms with you in your purse! Do not leave them in cars where temperatures can frequently change. Make sure you carry more than one! Take out your condoms and check expiration dates *before* a sexual encounter. (I know no one wants to do that in the moment, so prepare yourself.) When you pull out

a condom, take your index and thumb and press down on the wrapper. There should be an air bubble in the package. If there is no air bubble, that means the condom has been compromised and has a hole somewhere in the wrapper. Immediately throw away that condom.

2. It's not that sexy to open the condom with your teeth and slide it on his penis with your mouth. It may be used in porn, but practically, it can cause problems (for example, you can bite the condom and cause it to break). Instead you should use other types of sexual foreplay during this process. Whether it be touching yourself, looking into your partner's eyes, or taking off your clothes. Find an alternative method of creating sexual excitement while putting a condom on.

3. Use lube. It is important to use lube with a condom because a condom can break much easier if there is friction. There is lube that lasts twenty-four hours that you can put inside the vagina before going out on a date. Also travel-sized packages of lube are great to keep near the condoms in your purse.

THE IMPORTANCE OF USING BIRTH CONTROL

"If you aren't protecting, you're expecting."

There is no one form of birth control that works for everyone, which is why there are many options and brands on the market. Ultimately it is not important which form you decide, but that you are using one that works for your body.

Not all forms of birth control impact your hormones like birth-control pills or IUDs. Condoms work well and do not introduce anything new to your system. A multitude of options are available when it comes to birth control, and I encourage you to discuss options with your doctor. Some women choose to go to a gynecologist for birth-control prescriptions, but this is something your primary care doctor is also able to provide. Please do not take any advice in this book about birth control without first consulting a physician.

Some people choose to use the rhythm method or have the man pull out before ejaculation. I do not recommend these methods because they leave room for error, and they do not prevent the semen found in precome from entering a woman's body.

Birth-Control Pill

The birth-control pill is a hormone pill that allows you to have vaginal intercourse with a 99.9 percent effectiveness rate against pregnancy when taken correctly. It is important that a woman take the pill daily and at the same time for it to be effective.

A majority of women take birth-control pills that contain both estrogen and progestin. Some women are on progestin-only pills. Birth-control pills work by preventing the eggs from leaving the ovaries and making cervical mucus thicker, which prevents sperm from reaching the eggs. Other forms of birth control that are similar to the pill include the patch and the NuvaRing.

IUD

An intrauterine device, or IUD, is a small device made of flexible plastic that gets placed in the uterus. Different forms of IUDs have different ways of prevent pregnancy by preventing the sperm from joining with the egg. IUDs are becoming more common for both women who have had children and those who have never had children.

The Morning-After Pill, Plan B, Emergency Contraceptive

If you use a condom, and it falls off or breaks, if you have a sexual encounter and do not use protection (not recommended due to chance of contracting a sexually transmitted infection), or if you forget to take your birth-control pill, you can use the morning-after pill. The morning-after pill is most effective if taken shortly after the unprotected sexual encounter. However, it can reduce the chance of an unwanted pregnancy for up to five days after unprotected sex. Emergency contraception works by holding off on releasing the egg so that the sperm cannot fertilize. It also may prevent the fertilized egg from attaching in the uterus.

Just to be clear, Plan B is not the abortion pill. It is a form of birth control that should be used when other birth-control methods fail. You do not want this to be your main form of birth control. If you are regularly sexually active, you should use condoms and be on another method of birth control such as the pill, patch, NuvaRing, or IUD.

Have the Safe-Sex Talk Without Being "Awkward"

Ladies, let's face it. Sometimes it's awkward to have the safe-sex talk. It may feel weird, especially if you have something that you must tell a potential partner. It's extremely important to know what points you want to cover during the safe-sex talk before discussing this with a future lover. Note that during this talk is the perfect time to discuss sexual boundaries with the person as well. Make sure you are clear about what is off-limits for you.

Information you need to have: Your last STI checkup date and the results from this test. Therefore, you should have had an STI checkup. Sex does not have to be a scary thing full of danger and disease, which is why testing is important. You should know where you are at and ask the same of your partner. If you or your partner has an STI, it is okay, but you will need to take different precautions.

Quick Examples of a Woman's Safe-Sex Talk

"Before we hook up, I want to check in with you about testing. I got tested for STIs in October of this year, and I have had one partner since then who is also STI-free. I had a full inspection done, and all my results came out negative—so I am completely clean. If you want, I have the doctor's papers to prove it. When's the last time you got tested?"

Wait for the person to respond. If this partner is also clean, you can add something about your boundaries at this time in the conversation.

For example, "I am so excited to hook up with you, and I would like to use is a condom. Just so you know, I have a strong boundary against anal sex, but I am good for other types of sexual touch. Is there anything I should know about you?"

"I'd love to hook up with you. I just wanted to talk about safe sex before so we know where we both stand. The last time I got tested was in September of this year, and I have not had any partners since that time. I wanted to let you know that I have HSV 1, which is herpes, and although I have no symptoms right now, I wanted to give you the information prior to us hooking up. I get cold sores when I am stressed out, and I usually can feel them coming on ahead of time. Now I feel great and don't have any outbreaks. With that being said, I think we should definitely use condoms. If you are all right with this, I would love to hook up with you. When is the last time that you were tested?"

Wait for the answer.

TRY THIS OUT

Ask your partner:

- *"What do you consider cheating?"*
- *"Is there a time in your life where your sexual boundaries were violated that I should know about?"*
- *"What have you learned in your life about safe-sex techniques?"*

CONCLUSIONS

Know your worth, and make sure that you take precautions with your boundaries and with your body. Learn to ask the important questions about sexually transmitted infections, and learn to discuss what are important boundaries for your sexual partner to respect. Do not be afraid to speak up because there could be consequences more extreme than awkwardness in the moment.

CHAPTER 5

BEYOND VANILLA SEX

DISCLAIMER: PLEASE DO not assume that the *only* way toward sexual self-knowledge is that you *must* engage in certain behaviors. Although some people may find fulfillment through the activities in Chapter 5, other people may have a much different experience. Women get so much pressure (from their partners and from society in a larger sense) to be sexual performers rather than to figure out what gives them authentic sexual pleasure. I do not want to add to a woman's thought process in the beginning of her sexual experience that she *must* go through a certain set of sexual experiences to be considered a sexual being. The reason I include the following is because these are viewed by some as their common sexual practices. Whether you engage in missionary or BDSM, none of your preferences make you weird or unusual.

ANAL SEX

Many people publicly scoff at the idea of anal sex. Yet you would be surprised at how many times it comes up in my therapeutic sessions because people are doing it incorrectly. The results are that anal sex can be pleasurable if you decide this is something you want to do, but it can be a horrible experience if you go into it as you would vaginal intercourse. The following should prove useful should you decide to engage in anal sex.

Prepare your body: Make sure your bowels are empty prior to receiving anal sex. You may want to shower and wash the anus. This could be something you do with a partner to build up the mood. When you are done

46

prepping for hygiene, make sure you use fingers or a sex toy to prep the anus for penetration. It would be best if you used a toy that is similar in diameter to the penis that will be doing the penetration. Because the anus doesn't lubricate like the vagina, use a bunch of lube...you will not regret it. Just like with vaginal sex, condoms are recommended.

Prepare mentally: Make sure there is no time rush on your sexual encounter. Anal sex may take longer than regular sex because the anus, unlike the vagina, does not naturally lubricate, so it is best to begin by going slowly. As the receiver of anal sex, you need to learn how to relax the muscles in the anus to enjoy the sensations.

The anus has two sets of sphincter muscles. Sometimes it is easier to relax the first set. When you push something into the anus, you need to be able to relax both sets of muscles or else you can encounter problems. Most people can relax the first set of muscles, and then when something gets inserted, the receiver will tense up and resist, preventing any further penetration. At this point your partner may continue to force the object (be it a penis or a sex toy) into the anus. I recommend that you do not force anything into the anus, but instead take time and use patience while allowing the second set of sphincter muscles to relax as you become more comfortable.

Make sure that you pick a position that is comfortable in which you can control the speed on the penetration the first time you engage in anal sex. The spooning position and female on top helps the woman control the action. When you have anal sex, and it feels good, make sure you are vocal about what is enjoyable and what is too much. Tell your partner if he should go slower or change the pressure.

PROSTATE STIMULATION

The anus can be a pleasurable part of the body, for both men and women, and you can include it without engaging in anal sex. The prostate is located inside the male body and can be a source of extreme pleasure. Make sure that the man's bowels are empty and the anus is clean. Begin by rubbing the perineum (the area between the bottom of the testicles and the anus). Ask him to direct what type of pressure and touch is pleasurable. Once you are both comfortable, use water-based lube, and gently direct your fingers back toward the anus. While your male partner is lying on his back, move a finger into the anus about an inch or two and gently press upward. You should feel a round cluster of tissue, which is the prostate. Do the "come here" motion and ask him if this feels good. If it does not, massage the prostate with the pressure and movement he desires. Make sure to massage with the pads of your fingers and not with your nails. Once he is enjoying this sensation, ask him what he wants you to do with his penis to increase the pleasure. It is possible for men to orgasm through prostate stimulation alone, yet most find it more enjoyable to involve oral sex on the penis during prostate stimulation.

SQUIRTING

You've heard of it, but maybe you've never done it. Or you did it once, and you're not sure how it happened. Or maybe you do it all the time, but you don't know how to control it. Let's break down how female ejaculation (known as "squirting") occurs.

Usually squirting occurs when a woman is already at a certain level of heightened pleasure and sensation. She has already had an orgasm (a moment ago or ten minutes ago, it all depends) and now her body is continuing to build off the feeling of pleasure. Instead of contracting her body in and clenching during orgasm, ejaculate occurs when the woman releases and relaxes her body following a buildup of pleasure.

If you want to achieve a squirting orgasm, this is some of what you and your partner need to know. First, it can get messy. Put down a towel because you may expel a lot of liquid. Tell your partner to stimulate the clitoral gland externally with the tongue or fingers. Once you have had a regular orgasm, have your partner insert one finger in the vagina, palm facing up. Your partner can continue to move this finger in and out of the vagina while still putting pressure on the clitoral gland. Putting a thumb on the clit while sliding two fingers into the vagina can be a good preliminary move to help a woman squirt. While this happens the bulbs of the clit are filling internally, and the fingers inside the vagina are causing stimulation on the clitoris from the inside. The fingers should continue to move in and out of the vagina and to the left and right. The "come here" motion against the G-spot inside the vagina can be pleasurable; however, some women have reported that this becomes annoying and can inhibit them from squirting. If it does not work for you, that's okay. The key is to apply pressure on the clit on the outside and strong pressure on the inside of the vagina, hitting the back of the clit at the same time. The pressure of the finger motion, more so than the speed, is important for squirting. When you feel as though you are going to pee, this is a good sign. Instead of clenching in, release out. You will feel a rush of sensation and a surge of warmth. From what I have read, most women can squirt, but it does not mean that every woman will. For some women it will take practice to learn to release their bodies in a way that allows squirting to occur.

SPANKING

Sometimes it is super sexy to get a spank on the ass as you walk by a lover. It is a little love pat or a sign of the fun that is to come. What about if you stepped up the spanking and made it part of kinky play?

A bare-handed spank on the bottom can be extremely pleasurable, and it can be a good start to kinky play. While having sex from behind, you can have a partner slap your ass lightly and see how you like it. Have your lover do it again on the opposite side with the same pressure. Go back and forth with sides and even pressure. If you want more, you can ask for it harder.

Make sure that the spanks are on the full part of your bottom. The top, middle, and lower parts of your ass are all cushioned and can bring pleasure when a hand contacts them. Even your upper thighs underneath your rump can be hit and still bring pleasure!

If you become a big fan of this and your sex partner is willing, ask to engage in spanking as foreplay before you touch genitals. You can start with hand over clothes and then move down to bare-bottom spanking. Spank until the cheeks get rosy or your partner's hand hurts. Too much spanking can leave marks, so beware! This isn't necessarily a bad thing, but be careful if this is not what you are looking for.

WHAT IS BDSM?

BDSM is an acronym used to signify bondage/discipline, dominance/ submission, and sadism/masochism. It involves the act of role playing, power exchange, and sometimes inflicting pain on other consenting adults.

KINKY SEX

Stepping away from vanilla sex (standard or conventional sexual encounters) is thrilling and terrifying at the same time, especially if you don't know what you are doing. I am going to do my best at bringing you up to speed on Kink 101.

What do you need for a kink scene?

1. Consent. All adults involved (eighteen or older!) must give their verbal consent to engage in kink play.
2. Communication. Use your words when discussing boundaries and desires. Do not assume that the other person or people involved in play like exactly what you like. This is especially true if you are going to try to incorporate kink into your vanilla relationship.
3. Trust. The most important basis for engaging in any play with a partner is that you trust the person with whom you are playing. You need to trust that the person will comply with your wishes and desires and listen to you if you want to stop the scene.

How to Set Up a Kink Scene

A "scene" is the term that people use to describe a scenario or sexual play where they are engaging in kinky sexual activities.

To create a scene, all consenting adults must be on board with the plan. It is extremely important that everyone willingly wants to be involved in the scene and that no one is forced against his or her will to engage in play. Trust me—things can go extremely poorly when someone panics or is in over his or her head while in a kinky scene. If a partner does not communicate clearly about what he or she needs, it can be scary to all people involved when things go awry.

Remember the boundaries discussed earlier in the book? Recall those skills here. Know what brings you pleasure and what is a limit that you will not cross. Find safe words to use that slow down play if it is too intense or stop play completely if it is too much. Easy safe words to use are "yellow," meaning slow down the play, or "red," meaning stop what you are doing immediately.

Power Dynamics in Kink Scenes

One thing to note about kink scenes is that you can use intentional power play. In play between two people, usually one person has the control, and one person is relinquishing power to the other. Again all members involved agree to this, and thus it is the exchange in power that creates certain exciting dynamics of the kink scenes. Usually in scenes there is a "top" and a "bottom." The top has the control during the scene, and the bottom is giving up control and trusting the top to organize the logistics of how the sexual activity is going to go.

Try This Out

1. *Write a list of your sexual fantasies.*
2. *Try to write a sexy story for your eyes only.*

3. *Ask your partner if they would be interested in doing a role play this up-coming weekend. An example would be a job interview that becomes an erotic situation or you can pretend to be the aggressor if you usually wait for your partner to initiate.*

CONCLUSIONS

No matter if you are engaging in vanilla or kinky sex, it is important to know your body, communicate with your partner, and set clear boundaries. Discuss what feels pleasurable and where you are uncomfortable. Doing this will help make all sexual situations more comfortable. Try out new sexual activities only if everyone involved is interested. If you are not interested in trying anything in this segment of the book, know that you do not need to engage in any of these to be sexually fulfilled.

CHAPTER 6

CONCLUSION

I WROTE THIS book to bring women, especially younger women, positive information about finding their sexual identities. Crucial to this is the importance of acceptance, self-love, boundaries, and open conversation between partners so that women can experience true intimacy. The most important thing I have realized in my field is that simply talking to others about their sexuality has led to them experiencing deeper levels of intimacy with their partners.

Many times I think, "Why don't more people openly talk this way? What silences us? Is it shame or is it society?" The truth is that it doesn't matter. What does matter is the impact and ripple effect that can happen when individuals, specifically women, stop silencing themselves and open themselves up to self-love and their authentic voice. More so than just teaching sexual facts to others, I hope to encourage you to talk to people about their sexuality. If you can continue the conversations and spread the idea of intimacy to others, I believe there can be a great change within the erotic culture.

Yes, you may still have a good deal of unanswered questions. You must communicate with your partner to figure out how to have a great sexual exchange with each another. This book is a starting point to begin those conversations. It is great to know how often your partner likes to have sex or where that person likes to be touched, but know that it varies greatly moment to moment and partner to partner. I promise you that through talking with your partner, there is a chance of having great freedom within your intimate moments. So...let the conversations begin!

www.ingramcontent.com/pod-product-compliance
Lightning Source LLC
Chambersburg PA
CBHW072211090426
42740CB00012B/2487